THE
ALLIGATOR
AND THE EVERGLADES

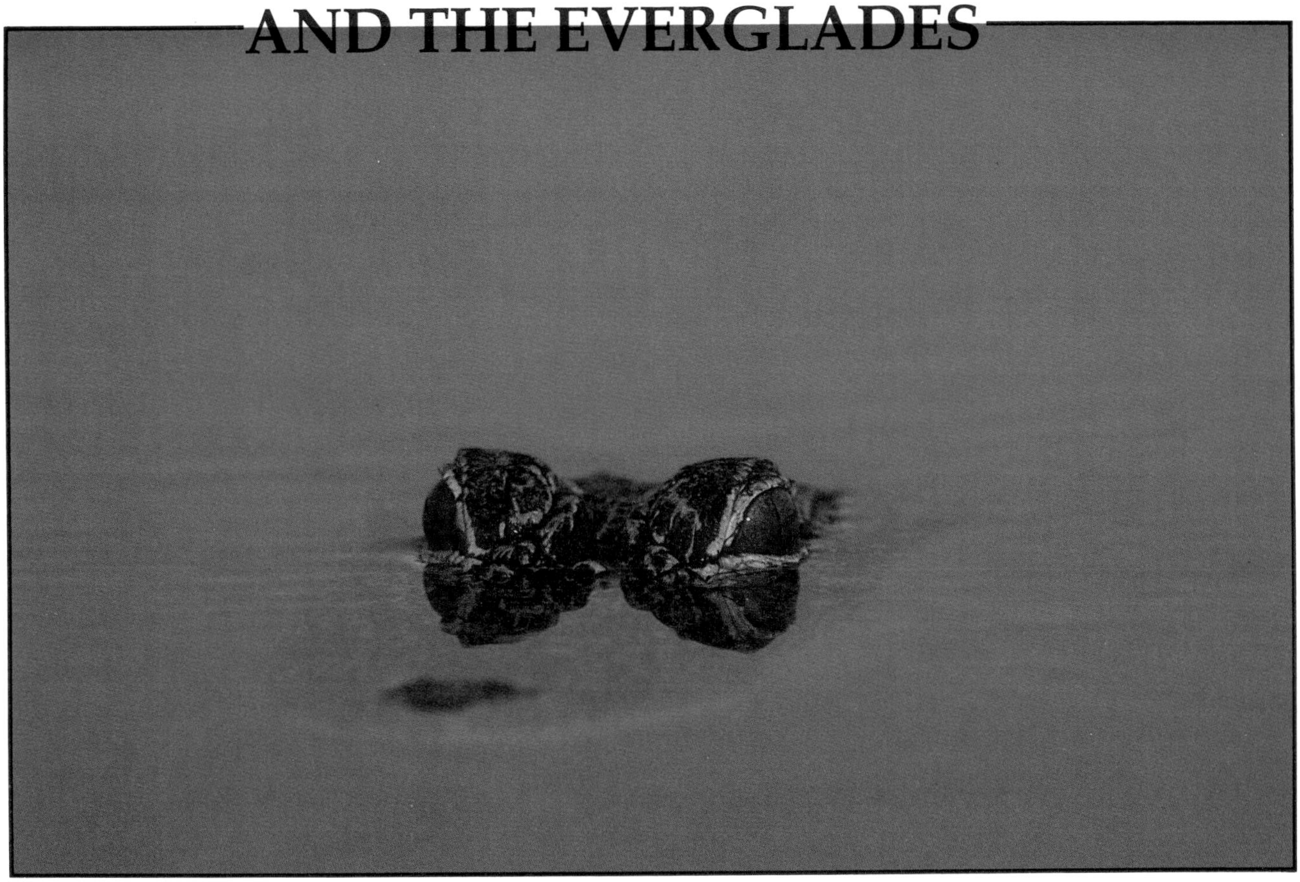

Text and photographs
Dave Taylor

Animals and their Ecosystems Series

Crabtree Publishing Company

A
Bobbie
Kalman
Book

Animals and Their Ecosystems Series
Dave Taylor

Editor-in-Chief
Bobbie Kalman

Editors
Christine Arthurs
Marni Hoogeveen
Janine Schaub

Design and pasteup
Adriana Longo

**All photographs by Dave Taylor except
the following:**
Animals Animals / Terry Slocum: p. 19 inset;
Animals Animals / Patricia Caufield: p. 27 bottom;
World Wildlife Fund: p. 28.

For Anne

I am especially grateful to the naturalists at
the Ding Darling Refuge and the Nature
Center on Sanibel Island for their help and
guidance. I am also appreciative of those
in South Carolina who took the time to
show me their gators.

350 Fifth Ave	1110 Kamato Road	73 Lime Walk
Suite 3308	Unit 4	Headington
New York	Mississauga, Ontario	Oxford 0X3 7AD
NY 10118	Canada L4W 2P3	United Kingdom

Contents

4   **Introducing Seminole**

6   **The constant crocodilians**

9   **A cold-blooded animal**

10   **The perfect predator**

12   **Alligator facts**

14   **The Everglades: a river of grass**

16   **Mating in the swamp**

18   **Baby gators everywhere**

20   **Mammal neighbors**

22   **A bounty of birds**

24   **Reptile relatives**

26   **Keystone species**

28   **Danger to the alligator**

30   **The alligator today**

32   **Glossary and Index**

Introducing Seminole

The swamp appears quiet and calm. Only the sound of the river grass rustling in the wind interrupts the silence of the hot afternoon. In the center of the river floats what looks like a bumpy log. Suddenly a pair of eyes appears, and the log starts to move. The log is not a log at all—it is an alligator in disguise! The gator swims slowly beside the bank of the river, paddling along with webbed feet. He is ten feet (three meters) long and still growing. His swamp home is part of The Everglades, a region in southern Florida. We shall name this young male after the Seminole, a group of native people who once lived in The Everglades.

Part of the family

Seminole is one of two alligator species existing in the world today. The smaller species lives in China and the larger species, to which Seminole belongs, lives in southeastern North America. Alligators belong to the order of animals known as crocodilians. Caimans, gavials, and crocodiles are also crocodilians. All these animals are part of a much larger group known as reptiles. Animals such as turtles, snakes, and lizards are reptiles. Instead of having hair, all these animals are covered with scales or hard protective plates. Some reptiles live only on land, whereas others live in water. They all, however, breathe air because they have lungs. Although Seminole is adapted to life on land, he spends most of his time in the shallow water.

The constant crocodilians

At one time reptiles dominated the earth. Dinosaurs, crocodilians, and other reptiles first populated the world around two hundred million years ago. They flourished in the many shallow seas as well as on land. In prehistoric times dinosaurs were the largest animals on earth. The crocodilians were smaller than most of the dinosours, but the dienosuchus, the largest of the crocodilians, was a huge animal. At over fifty feet (sixteen meters), it was as long as three full-grown elephants standing in a row! Today the largest crocodilians only grow to twenty feet (six meters) in length.

The Great Dying

Sixty-five million years ago something drastic happened that caused most of the animals on earth to die. Many species, including dinosaurs, became extinct, disappearing forever from the earth. This period is known as The Great Dying, yet no one knows for sure what happened. Perhaps an asteroid crashed into the earth, or the world became too cold. Perhaps a disease swept through the animal world or the sea level changed. Whatever happened, only the smaller crocodilians, birds, fish, and a few species of mammals managed to survive.

Still the same

As time went by, many animals developed and changed, but crocodilians did not. After millions of years crocodilians still have long bodies, big mouths full of sharp teeth, and huge tails. They still have short, powerful legs with webs between their clawed toes and hard horny plates, which form regular patterns on their backs, providing excellent protection. Seminole looks much like his crocodilian ancestors that walked the earth with the tyrannosaurus and the rest of the dinosaurs.

No competition

Crocodilians stayed the same because there was no great need for them to change. Fortunately, they did not have to compete with other animals for food. As predators, crocodilians hunted in order to survive. In the swamps and rivers where they made their homes, no other predators existed. If there had been other animals preying on the same creatures for food, crocodilians might have changed physically in order to outdo their competition. If a larger predator had hunted crocodilians, there would have been a need to become faster and smarter to avoid getting caught. Other animals had to contend with these problems, so they changed; crocodilians did not, so they stayed the same.

Even today Seminole has little competition in his watery world. Predators such as wolves, bears, lions, tigers, and hyenas hunt on dry land. Sharks, killer whales, and other sea predators stay out in the ocean. Only the river otter competes with the alligator for the same food, but the alligator far outnumbers this animal.

A stable climate

All crocodilians live in stable climates in the tropical, subtropical, and temperate regions of the world. These regions are close to the equator, where the temperature stays warm all year. The warm weather has not changed for centuries, so crocodilians have not had to adapt to different climates.

Most crocodilians need to live in a hot climate, so they are confined to the earth's tropical zones. The alligator, on the other hand, needs a subtropical or temperate climate, one that is not extremely hot or cold. Both the American alligator and its Chinese cousin live farther away from the equator than any of their crocodilian relatives.

All the animals on this page belong to the ancient crocodilian family. The Nile crocodile (above) is a true crocodile. It has a pointed snout, whereas the Chinese alligator (right) and the American alligator (below) both have shorter, rounded snouts.

A cold-blooded animal

The adjective "cold-blooded" is sometimes used to refer to heartlessness in human beings. When used to describe animals, however, it defines a physical condition. Like all reptiles, alligators are cold-blooded, which means they cannot automatically control their body temperatures. This characteristic makes them quite different from mammals and birds, which are warm-blooded animals. Food provides warm-blooded animals with the energy they need to stay warm. Whether the climate is hot or cold, warm-blooded animals maintain a constant body temperature.

The temperature of a cold-blooded animal, on the other hand, is greatly affected by its surroundings. On a cool day, an alligator's body cools off; on a hot day, it becomes very warm. This creates some problems. For instance, an alligator cannot live in a really cold climate because it would quickly freeze to death. It cannot survive in a really hot climate, either, because its blood would get too hot and boil its brains!

Basking in the sun

During the day alligators raise their body temperatures by soaking up the sun's warmth. Throughout the morning they warm up by lying on logs and riverbanks. If they get too hot later in the day, they cool off in the water. On cold summer nights alligators stay in the water, which has been warmed all day by the sun. By keeping warm, they can digest their food much more easily.

While soaking in the shallow water, Seminole still feels hot, so he opens up his huge mouth to cool it in the breeze. The air dries the moisture on Seminole's mouth and tongue which, in turn, cools off his blood. When you lick your finger and then blow on it softly, you notice that it feels cool. In the same way, alligators open their jaws and let the breeze cool down their big, wet mouths. Alligators can open their jaws very wide, increasing the area over which evaporation can take place. In order to lower his body temperature, Seminole sometimes pants like a dog!

Snoozing in the den

Even though the swamp normally has a temperate climate, Seminole occasionally faces life-threatening changes in the weather. How does he survive? In winter when the temperature can drop near the freezing point, alligators retreat into dens. An alligator makes its den under the roots of a tree on a riverbank or burrows a cozy cave at the end of a long tunnel. Because the den is under a blanket of soil, the temperature does not change much on cold or hot days. The earth insulates the animal against the weather outside, so it can sleep through both cold and hot spells. During cold spells Seminole becomes rather dozy because his blood cools and slows down. If the cold spell lasts a long time, he goes into his den and sleeps until the weather warms up.

A long time between meals

Being cold-blooded gives alligators a welcome advantage. They do not have to eat very much or very often. Warm-blooded birds and mammals may be able to survive in colder temperatures than reptiles, but they require a lot of food to keep warm. A gator consumes less than one fifth of the amount of food that a warm-blooded cougar of the same weight requires. An alligator keeps warm in the sun, so it does not need as much food. This means that the gator can afford to wait patiently for its prey to come by.

(top, left) Seminole peeks out from his den.

(top, right) Gators like to bask in the morning sun.

(bottom) In order to cool themselves, alligators open their jaws just as this American crocodile is doing.

The perfect predator

Although he is a good swimmer, Seminole seldom has to chase after his dinner. Instead, he surprises his victims by hiding and waiting quietly for the unwary prey to come to him. As he waits, only his protruding eyes and nostrils appear above the water. These special features allow him to remain almost invisible. His coloring also aids in disguising him. His dark bumpy body can be easily mistaken for a floating log. This technique of blending into surroundings is called camouflage. If Seminole wants to be out of sight completely, he sinks below the surface. Because he has a set of clear eyelids, he can still use his expert sense of sight underwater. If the water is muddy, he finds his prey by sensing its movements in the water. He can hold his breath underwater for nearly an hour.

Alligators are most active at night when their eyes are very sensitive to light. During the day their narrow pupils are closed almost completely. Although they appear to be snoozing lazily on the muddy banks of rivers, they are, in fact, quietly waiting for prey.

Seminole hunts a duck

Sometimes Seminole hunts by quietly drifting. He floats towards his prey until he is close enough for a quick and deadly charge. Today Seminole is hiding among the grasses at a bend in the river. After a short wait, a pair of unsuspecting ducks starts swimming towards him. They think he is a piece of rotting wood, so they are not afraid. As soon as they are within reach, however, Seminole attacks. He catches one duck and holds it underwater until it drowns. The other flies off, quacking loudly.

Good or bad?

Although we may be saddened that a duck has lost its life, we should remember that Seminole is not being cruel. Hunting is his way of staying alive. As a predator Seminole has an essential role to play in nature. Predators keep small animals from overpopulating a habitat and eventually destroying it.

(above) Only Seminole's eyes and nostrils show above the water's surface as he quietly waits for a pair of ducks to approach.

Fast in the water and on land

Seminole can move very quickly through the water by using his powerful tail. His short legs stay close to his body as he swishes his thick tail back and forth, pushing himself along. In short spurts, Seminole can also move very quickly on land—almost as fast as a horse! Gators can quickly dart up riverbanks to overtake prey that ventures too close to the pond.

Mighty jaws and terrible teeth

Seminole is ideally suited for his role as a predator. He has sharp teeth, some of which show even when he closes his lipless mouth. The muscles in his powerful jaws are very strong. Once he has clamped onto a leg or a tail, the victim has little chance of escaping. Seminole, like all alligators, is armed with eighty teeth. Until he stops growing, his new teeth replace the old ones once or twice a year. Old alligators lose more and more teeth until they can no longer hold onto prey. Then they slowly starve to death.

(above) Seminole kills a duck by grabbing it and holding it underwater until it drowns.

A gator's teeth are shaped like cones with very sharp points. This shape is perfect for grabbing and holding onto prey. Seminole's teeth are not good for chewing. He cannot move his jaws from side to side in a grinding manner. Instead, he swallows his prey whole or in large chunks. If the catch is too big to swallow, Seminole tears it apart by holding it in his jaws while spinning and thrashing about in the water. If he is too full to finish his meal, he drags it back to his den. If the prey is very large, he leaves it until it rots. It will then be soft enough to tear into smaller pieces.

Anchors aweigh!

After finishing his meal, Seminole swims to the bank of the river, picks up a few stones in his teeth, and swallows them. Do alligators eat stones? Not exactly. The stones stay in Seminole's stomach and act as an anchor. The weight of the stones helps him stay submerged underwater while hunting. Some scientists believe that these stones, called gastroliths, also help alligators grind and digest the food they have swallowed whole. Not all scientists agree with this second theory.

Alligator facts

Animal families

In order to better understand the world around us, scientists have divided plants and animals into groups of related species. American alligators, known officially as *Alligator mississippiensis,* belong to the crocodilian family. Crocodilians are part of the order of animals commonly known as reptiles.

Crocodilians

There are three groups of crocodilians: the alligators and caiman, the gavial, and the true crocodiles. The caiman, which belongs to the alligator family, is much smaller than the alligator and lives in South America. The gavial has an extremely long snout, with more than a hundred teeth. The largest family of crocodilians, the true crocodiles, have thirteen species in their group. At first glance it is difficult to tell alligators and crocodiles apart. Crocodiles have long, thin snouts, whereas alligators have rounded ones. When alligators and crocodiles close their mouths, it is easy to tell them apart. Alligators only show their top teeth, whereas crocodiles show all their teeth.

Feet and toes

Alligators have five long toes on their front feet, which give them a firm footing on land. Their back feet have only four toes, but they are webbed, which helps gators steer in the water.

Alligators spend much of their day lying in wait for prey to get close enough to catch.

Protective flaps and lids

The ear openings of an alligator have special flaps that allow the ears to close underwater. When a gator dives, he closes his nostril flaps and throat to stop the water, but he cannot close his mouth. Without lips, water pours into the gator's mouth, but never gets past its closed throat. Alligator eyes have vertical pupils, which ensure excellent night vision. They are protected by three eyelids: one above, one below, and one at the side of the eye. The side one, called a nictitating membrane, moves sideways across the eye and cleans its surface just as a windshield wiper cleans a window. This lid is so thin and clear that the alligator can see right through it.

Where did that alligator go? Only a few animals are so well adapted to life on both land and water.

Guarding the young

Most reptiles abandon their eggs once they have laid them. Alligators do not. They guard their eggs until they hatch and sometimes stay close by for up to three years. There is no need for the mother to worry about feeding her young, however. Baby gators are able to catch their own food as soon as they hatch.

Although water flows in and out of the mouths of crocodilians, special valves close off their throats.

A ride among sharp teeth

It has recently been discovered that a mother alligator digs into her nest when she hears the croaking of her infants inside their eggs. When the eggs hatch, the mother gathers the babies in her mouth and carries them to nearby water for their first swim. The offspring stay together near the nesting site for some time.

Changing tastes

Young alligators eat insects and shellfish such as crabs and shrimp. As they grow, their diets include fish, snakes, and frogs. Young adults progress to eating bigger animals such as birds, raccoons, muskrats, fish, and mammals that happen to cross their paths.

Is it a log? Is it a gator? The alligator uses its camouflage to hide among the river debris.

Using the liver to breathe

An alligator breathes by moving its liver back and forth. When the liver is moved backwards, air is sucked into the lungs. Moving the liver forward expels the air from the lungs.

Powerful jaws

Alligators have large jaw muscles that help them crack the bones of their prey. These muscles are powerful only when clamping down, however. The muscles that open the jaws are feeble by comparison.

Evil dragons?

In the past, people feared alligators because they thought of them as dragons or prehistoric monsters that loved to eat people. Alligators may look frightening, but they do not especially like to eat people. Alligators are capable of killing human beings, but they are responsible for only a few such attacks. They much prefer hunting smaller prey. Because alligators are predators, people sometimes think of them as evil creatures. Ali predators, including alligators, are essential to the ecosystems in which they live. They keep other species of animals in check by hunting them.

The Everglades: a river of grass

One of the places where alligators thrive is The Everglades. The Everglades is a huge marsh, which is an area of low, wet land where grasses, rushes, and sedges thrive. The water in the marsh is actually a broad, slow-moving river that flows over a limestone bottom and drains into the ocean. In most places the water is only six inches (fifteen centimeters) deep and barely moves.

Tall grasses that grow from the river bottom can be seen in every direction. There are also many islands called hummocks, which are small areas of land that are just above the water line. A hummock can support a whole jungle of plants. In other spots fresh water bubbles up from springs in the limestone riverbed.

A swampy home

Seminole makes his home in a swampy area of The Everglades. Here the land is not quite as wet. There are ponds and streams, but trees as well as grasses can grow in the mucky ground. Seminole's swamp is filled with tall cypress trees and dangling Spanish moss.

Parts of an ecosystem

Seminole's swamp is part of The Everglades ecosystem. An ecosystem is a community made up of living and non-living parts. The non-living parts include the soil, rocks, water, gases in the air, and energy from the sun. These parts make up the physical environment. The living community includes the vegetation of the area and the insects, birds, and all the other animals, including Seminole.

A great variety of grasses

Grass seems to grow everywhere in The Everglades. Hundreds of grass species thrive in this moist ecosystem, including beard grass, marsh fleabane, lovevine, creeping Charlie, and ludwigia. Saw grass, a type of sedge that has a solid stem, grows to a height of thirteen feet (four meters). It is slim and narrow and has the typical blade shape of grass, though it is not a true grass. Rushes grow in the shallow water, where thinner soil is found. Their stalks are round, hollow, and smooth to the touch.

The Everglades is a broad, shallow river.

Collecting food energy

In The Everglades the grass is the foundation of the ecosystem because it is the main producer. As a producer grass is able to take in energy from the sun and transform it into food energy for the animals that eat it. Animals and insects are unable to make their own energy. They are consumers because they must get their food energy either directly or indirectly from plants. Plant-eating animals, known as herbivores, receive their food energy directly from plants. Carnivores, or meat-eating animals, get their food energy indirectly. They eat herbivores or other animals that eat herbivores, which in turn get their food energy from plants.

An interconnected community

The system by which energy is passed along in an ecosystem is called a food chain. Many food chains form a food web. Plant- and algae-eating insects abound in the marsh food web. Insects are eaten by small carnivores such as spiders, fish, frogs, and crayfish, which are, in turn, eaten by other animals such as raccoons. They are eventually eaten by larger carnivores such as the alligator. The waste material produced by the animals returns nutrients to the soil to help the grasses grow. Insects and fungi, called decomposers, help break down these materials into basic forms so they can be reused. Nothing is wasted in an ecosystem that is left in its natural state.

Adapting to wet and dry

To most of the world the pine tree is associated with the far north, but pines also flourish in parts of the gator's range. Pine needles are leaves that are specially adapted to allow trees to keep their moisture for long periods of time. The moisture-conserving pine trees flourish in sandy soil that cannot hold water. In the swamp where Seminole lives, trees must contend with too much water. The cypress tree solves this problem by growing "knees" to support it in the wet, mushy ground. Other trees support themselves by sending archlike roots in all directions.

Two types of palm trees grow in the alligator's range. Fanleaf palms, above, have leaves with rounded outlines. Featherleaf palms have long leaves. The Spanish moss, right, hangs from swamp trees and gets its food energy totally from the surrounding air. Below, grass grows in abundance in the marsh.

Mating in the swamp

When the hot weather arrives in March, alligator bulls test one another to see which males are bigger and stronger than the others. They do this by pushing and wrestling. After a winner emerges, they do not fight again. The strong males win the best territories. Weak males must be satisfied with areas that do not have good food or water sources. Seminole tests his strength against other gators his size. Because he is not fully grown, he does not dare challenge any huge bulls.

After bellowing all night long, Seminole patrols his territory.

Proclaiming territories

Bellowing is a good way for male gators to proclaim their territories. A bellow sounds much like a stalling outboard motor. It can be heard by gators far across the wetlands. Bellowing helps limit serious fighting between alligators. Male alligators usually stay away from a territory in which they have heard a bellowing bull. Should a stranger ignore the warning and enter the territory, the resident gator hisses at the intruder and chases it away. Seminole and the other males and females in his area make bellowing noises all year round.

Noisy mating calls

Early in the spring mating season, the alligators begin their courtship rituals. Their mating bellows are especially noisy. Males bellow to let females know where they are. Seminole vibrates the air column in his mouth, filling the swamp night with his gruff-sounding mating calls. During mating season, his musk glands give off a strong, sweet smell, which also attracts females to his territory.

Tough love

A female enters Seminole's territory and tests Seminole's strength by shoving him around and pushing him underwater. She will not mate with young males that are still small and weak. Although not yet fully grown, Seminole is strong enough to convince the female that he can provide her with healthy offspring.

After much coughing and splashing, Seminole and his partner engage in a variety of mating rituals. They slap the water with their heads and rub each other's muzzles and necks. They also grunt at each other and bellow loudly. Eventually they mate in shallow water.

An independent lifestyle

Although they stay in their territories, males breed with several females. Unlike males, female alligators do not have territories. They move wherever they like and mate several times. A female is ready to mate in mid-April and travels around until the mating season ends in May. Once a male and female have bred, they have nothing further to do with each other.

(above) Before accepting Seminole as a mate, the female gator pushes against his side to test his strength.

Baby gators everywhere

Female alligators lay their eggs in nests. In June they partially build several nests before they decide which one to use. Why alligators make these false starts at building nests is a mystery, but perhaps they are not satisfied with the locations of the first ones. Seminole's mate wants the nest to be on high ground so that it does not flood when the water rises. She picks a shady spot to protect her eggs from the hot summer sun. Finally satisfied, she completes the nest.

Making a nest

The female gator uses her body, legs, and tail to make the nest from sand, soil, and rotting vegetation. The decaying vegetation produces heat, which keeps the eggs warm. The alligator spends about two weeks building her nest. When she is finished, it is between eighteen and thirty inches (forty-five and seventy-five centimeters) high and up to seven feet (two meters) across. With her hind feet she digs a hole in the middle of the mound and lines it with mud. When she is ready, she lays between twenty and seventy eggs and then covers them up. An alligator's white eggs are about twice the size of chicken eggs, but they are not the same shape. The ends of alligator eggs are of equal size.

Patiently waiting

Sixty to seventy days pass before the eggs hatch. Throughout this time the mother gator is never very far from her nest. She cannot hunt because she spends her time protecting the unhatched young from egg-loving predators such as the raccoon, gray fox, and skunk. When it is time for the eggs to hatch, the tiny reptiles start chirping inside the eggs. The mother hears these noises, so she uncovers the eggs. With the help of a horny tip on the snout, called an egg tooth, the young gators break open their shells. In her mouth Mom carries the lizard-like babies to the water. They are able to swim the minute they hatch.

Timed hatchings

Most of the female gators that live in one area lay their eggs at the same time. Their eggs hatch at approximately the same time, too. Nature does this for a reason. Many predators eat defenseless newborns. With so many baby alligators running and swimming about at one time, predators are unable to capture all of them. Even though timed hatchings improve a baby alligator's chances of survival, only one in ten lives to the end of its first year.

Baby gators in distress

At ten inches (twenty-five centimeters) long, baby alligators are too small to defend themselves. Because they are brightly colored with black and yellow stripes, predators can spot them quite easily. Fortunately baby alligators make a lot of noise when they are in danger. By chirping loudly, a youngster warns its brothers and sisters that there is an enemy nearby. The siblings quickly dive for shelter. The loud chirps also bring adult alligators to the area to protect the babies. By the time the youngsters reach four years of age, they stop making distress calls and start responding to the calls of younger gators.

Seminole to the rescue!

Seminole lies sleepily sunning himself on the bank of the river, when suddenly he hears the "chirp, chirp, chirp" of a baby alligator in distress. His eyes open wide, and he gives a push with his legs, plunging down the bank on his belly. He swims quickly towards the captured youngster. At the nesting site, he spots a raccoon running with the chirping baby in its mouth. Seminole rushes over, but the raccoon runs up a tree just in time. Although he has arrived too late to help the captured baby, he has at least chased off a predator before it made away with any more victims. Losing interest, Seminole slides into the water to swim back to his sunning spot.

A raccoon startles some baby gators so they plunge into the water for safety. Seminole comes to their rescue when he hears a call of distress.

Growing gators

Alligators grow quickly up to the age of six years. At first they catch worms, bugs, snails, and dragonflies with their needle-like teeth. As they grow, they move on to tadpoles, frogs, small fish, crabs, and crayfish. When food is plentiful, male alligators grow about twelve inches (thirty centimeters) a year until they are fifteen years of age. Some bulls reach lengths of sixteen feet (five meters), but this is rare. Females stop growing at approximately eight years of age and rarely exceed ten feet (three meters) in length. Alligators occasionally live to reach fifty years of age.

Alligator nests are located on high ground. The nest materials help keep the eggs warm.

Mammal neighbors

The Everglades ecosystem, where Seminole's swamp is located, provides an abundance of food for small mammals. The grasses and many insects feed some mammals. They also ensure the presence of numerous small fish and birds, which are food for other mammals. Large mammals such as bears would have a hard time traveling in the water and muck, so most mammals in The Everglades are fairly small. Mammals such as rodents, raccoons, marsh rabbits, opossum, and armadillos all provide food for their natural enemy, the alligator.

Risky business

Raccoons are fond of the same small creatures upon which young alligators prey. The raccoon can often be seen searching along the shore for crabs and other small animals. This mammal is an opportunistic eater. It feeds on almost anything, whether animal or vegetable. It digs into alligator nests and eats as many of the tasty eggs as possible before the mother alligators return. Bird nests filled with eggs or newly hatched birds are another raccoon favorite. These nests are frequently located above water. Sometimes an over-eager raccoon ventures out on a limb, loses its balance, and falls into the water below. It may then become a meal for an alligator lurking below. A raccoon can also fall prey to a gator's sudden attack while swimming to distant islands looking for bird colonies.

The raccoon (left) and the opossum (below) both search for food along the water's edge, where the alligator sometimes catches them.

20

Marsh rabbits

The swamp seems an unlikely spot to find a rabbit, but one species of bunny flourishes here—the marsh rabbit. It is about the same size as the cottontail rabbit but lacks the distinctive white tail. Marsh rabbits are good swimmers, so they often swim to islands, tempted by the green grass. Naturally, as they swim across open water, they fall prey to submerged alligators. To maintain their population, they reproduce quickly and have many offspring.

The opossum

The opossum is North America's only marsupial. Marsupials have special pouches in which they carry their young. The opossum is an opportunistic eater like the raccoon. It spends most of its time searching for food in the trees. Occasionally it comes within reach of the gator's deadly jaws as it searches the water for food. Seminole sees a pair of opossum over by the river's edge. Although they look tempting, he does not attack the pair. They are too far away, and Seminole still feels full from a fish he ate for breakfast.

The rabbit (right) protects itself by running away, whereas the armadillo (below) curls up in a ball.

The armadillo

Both the opossum and armadillo came to North America from South America through Mexico. In the twentieth century the armadillo has slowly expanded its range eastward. This tanklike creature is fond of eating insects and grubs. It roots around in the forest debris in search of these tasty tidbits. Armadillos hide from predators by curling up into balls completely surrounded by their armor-like body plates. Even though the shell of an armadillo is tough, an alligator's jaws are powerful enough to crack one open.

21

A bounty of birds

Birds are plentiful in alligator country. They arrive in every size, shape, and color to enjoy the mild winter climate and take advantage of the bountiful supply of insects and small fish in Seminole's ecosystem. They leave once the warmer weather arrives in summer. As a result The Everglades experiences a constant ebb and flow of winged wildlife. Only the tropics have more species of birds than The Everglades.

(above) The brown pelican dives from the air and scoops up fish into the pouch under its bill.

The ahinga, or water turkey, swims so fast that the alligator cannot catch it. It spreads its wings to dry in the sun.

Roseate spoonbills catch tiny water creatures by filtering water through their specially adapted bills

(below) The egret is a frantic hunter. To stir up its prey, it runs through the water, wings outspread. Some egrets hunt the lizards that live in the long grasses near the water's edge.

Osprey, often called the fish hawk, compete with alligators for the fish that abound in the shallow water of The Everglades.

The leggy blue heron hunts by wading in the shallows. When it spots a meal, it draws up its neck, waggles its head from side to side, and then spears the fish with its beak.

Reptile relatives

Many reptiles share the alligator's ecosystem. Because reptiles can live on land or in water, they are well suited to life in The Everglades, a place that most animals find either too wet or too mucky. Reptiles include such species as turtles, snakes, and lizards. Instead of having hair, all these animals are covered with scales or hard protective plates. They lay eggs, have backbones, and breathe air because they have lungs. Reptiles are particularly well suited to the climate of The Everglades, which is not too hot and not too cold. Because they are cold-blooded, they like to be near the shallow water where they can either warm up or cool down.

Leaping lizards!

Many types of lizards inhabit Seminole's swamp. Lizards are famous for their ability to grow replacement tails if they lose their first ones. If one gets caught by the tail, it simply sheds the appendage and runs away! Slowly a new tail grows in to replace the lost one. The alligator can also grow back part of its tail if it is bitten off, but cannot shed it at will the way a lizard can. Most lizards feed on a variety of insects such as cockroaches, grasshoppers, beetles, and mosquitoes.

One of the fastest lizards in the world is the six-lined racerunner. It can run at about eighteen miles (thirty kilometers) per hour when it needs to. The green anole, another lizard, protects itself with its expert camouflaging skills. It can change the color of its skin to match the color of its surroundings. For instance, if it climbs a bright green tree, its skin turns from sandy brown to bright green. Sometimes the green anole is mistakenly called a chameleon, but true chameleons are only found in Africa and India.

The skink (left) and the green anole (below) are both lizards that live in the swamp. Even though these reptiles look similar to alligators, they are not close relatives.

Turtles, such as the soft-shelled turtle above, spend most of their time in water swimming using their webbed feet. Tortoises, such as this gopher tortoise, live on land and can dig in soil with their stumpy feet.

Turtles and tortoises

A great many turtles and tortoises live in the swamps and marshes of the south. Some of these are Mississippi sliders, soft-shelled turtles, and snapping turtles. Their close relative, the gopher tortoise, also lives in the swamp. The gopher tortoise prefers dry land and sunny days.

Although only the size of a dinner plate, the gopher tortoise affects the lives of several other species. Each tortoise digs a long burrow in which it lives. Many other animals use this burrow as a home, too. A tortoise might share its living quarters with an opossum, a marsh rabbit, a gray fox, or with crickets, mice, gopher frogs, and snakes. Without the tortoise many of these creatures would be unable to survive because the tortoise's burrow provides the only shelter from the hot sun.

The crocodile

The crocodile, a reptile similar to the alligator, has a long, thin snout rather than a rounded one. Crocodiles live in tropical climates rather than in the subtropical or temperate climate of the alligator's home. Whereas alligators are almost entirely freshwater creatures, crocodiles can be found in both freshwater and saltwater. Crocodiles live in places such as in the Nile River in Africa and along Australia's northern coast. A few crocodiles live in the southernmost part of the gator's range. They are serious competition for alligators because they eat the same foods. Seminole has seen only two crocodiles in his whole life!

Keystone species

Some animals play crucial roles in their ecosystems. Scientists use the term "keystone species" to identify animals that lend support to many of their animal neighbors. A keystone is the special stone in a wall that is placed in such a way that it keeps all the other stones from falling down. One keystone species is the gopher tortoise because its burrow provides a home for many other animals. The alligator plays such an important role in its ecosystem that it is also considered a keystone species. These two animals can be used to determine the health of their ecosystem. If the alligators in Seminole's swamp are flourishing, then scientists can be sure that many other species are doing well, too.

Digging water holes

The alligator is a keystone species because its presence provides food, water, and shelter for many animals. The major contribution the alligator makes to its ecosystem is the water holes it digs in the shallow marsh. Because alligators prefer deeper water, they dig big holes in the limestone riverbed. These holes are usually about twenty-six feet (eight meters) wide and eleven feet (three-and-a-half meters) deep. The water holes are cool places in which

the alligators and other animals can hide during the heat of the day. The dirt dug up from the bottom forms a bank all around the hole. Here trees and other plants are able to grow. Water holes provide two flourishing habitats, one on land and one in water, where many animals live.

During the rainy seasons of summer and fall the water level is high in The Everglades. Gator holes cannot be seen because they are out of sight below the surface of the water. In spring, however, the water all but vanishes in the marsh. Only the gator holes are still full of water. When the rest of the land is dry, the water holes serve as natural reservoirs. Plants and predators all rely on this life-giving water. The alligators and many other animals live comfortably in or near these wet depressions until the rainy weather returns.

Helping others

The holes that gators dig help people and domestic animals, too. Cattle ranchers who have numerous alligators on their properties know that gator holes provide water for their thirsty cattle. Ranchers who do not have gator holes on their properties must bring in water by truck for their livestock. People discovered another benefit of the gator holes only after they had disappeared. As the number of alligators decreased, so did their water holes. An overwhelming number of mosquitoes began biting local residents. This unpleasant turn of events occurred because there was no longer a place for the mosquito-eating fish to live. Now that people know the benefits of gator holes, they value the gators more. As long as Seminole and his fellow alligators are hunting and basking in the sun, we know that the river of grass supports a healthy population of all kinds of animals.

The gopher tortoise's burrow provides a home for many animals.

(below) Alligators dig deep holes in the limestone riverbed and push all the soil to the edge. Vegetation takes root in the soil and mosquito-eating fish (left) thrive in the deep water. These fish keep mosquitoes and many other annoying insects under control.

Danger to the alligator

For centuries The Everglades provided habitats for many species. Unfortunately, much of this marsh is now gone. At first people thought it was useless land because it was so wet they could not build on it or farm it. Huge concrete dams were built to drain large portions of the marsh for building and farming purposes. Canals and dikes also crisscross the area. The dams and canals prevent the water from flowing naturally into The Everglades. Not too long ago it seemed that many of the southern swamps would dry up completely. Without water the grasses dry out and can easily catch fire. If The Everglades disappeared, so would the water supply for the whole area. Fortunately, concerned people realized the dangers before it was too late. Steps were taken to repair some of the damage and make sure

enough water flowed to the home of the alligators. Happily, although the marsh is now smaller, it is in much better shape.

The leather trade

Lack of water and loss of habitat are only two of the threats faced by the alligator. About two hundred years ago the alligator population began shrinking because hunters killed many of these reptiles for their luxurious skins. Alligator skin is highly valued because, unlike the skin of most crocodilians, the belly leather is not full of armor-like bony plates called osteoderms. Fashionable shoes, belts, purses, and briefcases were made from fine-quality alligator leather.

(above) Alligator hides are made into shoes, belts, suitcases, and other fine leather goods.

The slaughter

It is believed that earlier this century nine million alligators were killed. Over one million were killed in The Everglades alone. In the 1960s alligator hunting became illegal, but the hunting continued. People who kill animals illegally are called poachers. Alligator poachers kept on hunting because the punishment was not strong enough to make them stop. The poachers received only a small fine for their illegal actions, so they did not mind taking the risk of getting caught. Meanwhile, they made large amounts of money selling the skins to people who were willing to pay high prices for them.

Endangered species

In the 1970s laws were passed that gave the alligator "endangered-species" status. A species is called endangered when so few animals are left that the animal is in danger of becoming extinct. Stricter laws were passed to protect the alligator from being hunted. The sale of alligator leather was banned in many countries. After these laws were passed, alligator numbers increased rapidly. Unlike his parents, Seminole has many alligator neighbors. Today there are enough alligators that some hunting is allowed once again. Licensed hunters can hunt wild alligators, but the harvest is carefully controlled so that the population will stay high. Handbags, shoes, and other alligator-skin products are again being sold in stores. This upsets many conservation groups that believe the alligator still needs complete protection.

Alligator farms

Today some alligators are raised on farms for their leather and meat. These farms provide a good source of alligator leather, so fewer people can make money poaching the wild population. As well as being a good method of preventing poaching, alligator farms could also be used to replenish the wild population if it ever became endangered again.

Gators fed by people can become demanding. Signs are used to warn people not to interfere with nature.

The alligator today

The alligator now lives in many places outside its normal ecosystem. The once-declining alligator population has been increasing, but the alligators have less space to call home because more and more land is being taken over by people. This means that many gators must leave the wilderness to inhabit freshwater ponds and lakes wherever they can find them. At times the alligator's search for water leads it to some bizarre and unusual places, especially during the dry season.

Uninvited guests

Alligators have been found in drainage ditches, sewers, cemeteries, parks, and even swimming pools. These excursions into neighborhoods have led to many strange encounters. Tall tales are sometimes told about alligators that come to barbecues as uninvited guests.

When their habitats are destroyed, alligators cross dry land to find new homes.

A golf hazard

Golfers throughout the alligator's range often find these giant reptiles in the ponds and creeks of golf courses. Players are warned not to retrieve a ball if it lands near one of these animals. Although the alligator is the least dangerous of the crocodilians, like all wild animals, it should be treated with caution. Today, largely because they are such a common sight in parks, zoos, and on golf courses, people think of them as harmless, lazy animals. Those who think of them as harmless may try to get too close. They forget that the carnivorous alligator has a strong biting instinct. In many areas feeding alligators has been banned altogether. These laws are meant to protect both human beings and reptiles. Most alligators, however, ignore humans, so people can feel fairly safe.

The magnificent alligator

Unlike the alligator, most crocodilians are not doing well. Poaching and fear cause the needless deaths of many of these ancient reptiles. Only the alligator seems assured of a future. In order to save its habitat, many parks and reserves have been established throughout the alligator's North American range. These parks are visited by millions of people each year. It is exciting to see these living "dinosaurs" up close. Visitors usually leave the parks convinced that the impressive alligator is well worth saving.

Seminole lies quietly at the river's edge soaking up the last rays of the evening sun. He does not know or care about humankind's concern over his welfare. He has a full belly, the sun feels warm, and life could not be better!

Because people have taken action to save The Everglades, Seminole is now free to live as nature intended.

Glossary

asteroid - A huge rock that floats in space
bellow - A loud, deep coughing sound alligators make to communicate with one another
camouflage - The color or pattern of an animal or object that helps it blend in with its surroundings
carnivore - A meat-eating animal
cold-blooded - Unable to generate body warmth. The body temperature of a cold-blooded animal changes to match its surroundings.
conservation - The act of protecting our natural resources, including animals, from being destroyed
crocodilian - A member of the largest family of reptiles
decomposer - An organism such as a worm, fungus, or bacteria that reduces what it eats into nutrients, which are then returned to the environment
ecosystem - The interdependent community of plants and animals and the surroundings in which they live
environment - The surroundings in which an animal or plant lives
endangered - Close to becoming extinct
extinct - Describing species that no longer exist
habitat - The area in which a plant or animal lives
herbivore - A plant-eating animal
instinct - A natural drive to act a certain way
keystone species - An animal whose presence lends support to other animals by providing necessities such as food, shelter, or water

mammal - An animal that is warm-blooded, covered in hair, and has a backbone. A female mammal has mammary glands that produce milk.
marsh - A low-lying area of land submerged by water
mating - The breeding of a male and female of a species
nutrient - A substance that a living thing consumes to be healthy and strong
opportunistic - Describing an animal that eats almost anything available, both plant and animal
poacher - A person who kills wild animals unlawfully
predator - An animal that hunts and kills other animals for food
range - An area of land where a species lives
reptile - An animal that is cold-blooded, lays eggs, breathes air, and is adapted to life on water and land
reserve - A protected area set aside for animals
subtropical - Describing climates or areas that are almost as hot and humid as the tropics
species - A distinct animal or plant group that shares similar characteristics and can produce offspring within its group
swamp - An area of wet, muddy land on which some trees grow
temperate - Describing climates or areas that do not become very hot or very cold
territory - An area of land an animal claims as its own
tropical - Describing a climate or an area near the equator that is hot and humid all year round

Index

ahingas 22
alligator holes 26, 27
alligator leather 28, 29
armadillos 20, 21
baby alligators 13, **18-19**
bellowing 16, 17
birds 6, 13, 20, **22-23**
blue herons 23
breathing 13
bulls 16, 19
caimans 5, 12
camouflage 4, 10, 13, 24
Chinese alligators 5, 6, 7
cold-blooded **8-9**, 24
conservation **28-29**, 31
crocodiles 5, 6, 7, 8, 9, 12, 25
crocodilians 5, **6-7**, 12, 28, 31
dens 8, 9, 11
dinosaurs 6, 31
ecosystems 13, **14-15**, 20, 22, 24, 26, 30
egg tooth 18

eggs 13, **18-19**, 20, 24
egrets 23
Everglades, The 4, **14-15**, 20, 22, 24, 26, 28, 29, 31
eyes 10, 12
feet 6, 12
food 6, 9, 11, 13, 19, 20
gavials 5, 12
Great Dying, The 6
hunting 6, **10-11**, 13, 26, 29
insects 13, 14, 15, 19, 20, 21, 22, 24
jaws 8, 11, 13, 21
keystone species **26-27**
lizards 5, 23, 24
mammals 6, 9, 13, **20-21**
marsh **14-15**, 26, 28
marsh rabbits 20, 21, 25
mosquitoes 26
mouths 9, 11, 12, 13, 17, 18
nests 13, **18-19**, 20

North America 5, 6, 21, 31
nostril flaps 12
opossums 20, 21, 25
osprey 23
pelicans 22
poaching 29, 31
predators 6, **10-11**, 13, 18, 21, 26
raccoons 13, 15, 18, 19, 20
reproduction **16-17**
reptiles 5, 6, 9, 12, 13, 18, **24-25**, 31
roseate spoonbills 22
size 19
sleeping 9
stomach stones 11
swamps 4, **14-15**, 20, 21, 24, 26, 28
tails 6, 11, 24
teeth 11, 13
territories **16-17**
tortoises 25, 26
turtles 5, 24, 25

1 2 3 4 5 6 7 8 9   WP Printed in the U.S.A.   9 8 7 6 5 4 3 2 1 0